THE BRIMMERS™ BOOK OF COCKTAILS

Enjoy!

Mike & Winnie

THE BRIMMERS™ BOOK OF COCKTAILS

Mike Palmer

First published in October 2017

ISBN 978-1-5272-1379-1

Book Typeset by **DigiConv Technologies Services Pvt. Ltd.**, New Delhi, India.

Contents

INTRODUCTION

I am an enthusiastic maker and drinker of cocktail bitters but I cannot claim to have been a lifelong devotee. It was not until 2011 that I discovered and quickly fell in love with bitters when my girlfriend, Jen, (now my wife) and I visited New Zealand, where Lemon Lime & Bitters (LLB) seemed as ubiquitous as Coca Cola. Since that time, I have derived great pleasure from finding cocktails whose recipes call for the inclusion of a few drops of these peculiar potions.

In 2014 I had the idea to craft my own bitters in my garage in rural Cambridgeshire, not knowing then that it would take the best part of three years to perfect the recipe. Whilst the fundamental process for producing bitters is quite simple – extracting essences from botanicals and spices using strong alcohol – the complexities of arriving at the right bitterness, sweetness, flavour combination and clarity were seemingly endless. In 2017, after countless trials, the recipe was finalised and Brimmers bitters was released to the cocktail making public.

Alongside sharing my creation with the world, I also wanted to collect in one place a set of cocktail recipes that (to some degree) call for the use of bitters. The recipes contained within these pages are by no means a comprehensive list and you would likely find hundreds more, were you to scour every bar across every continent. Nonetheless, this book does provide a broad introduction to a range of recipes from the UK, the USA, the Caribbean, Latin America, and even further afield.

Why Brimmers?

All the recipes contained within this book call for Brimmers bitters. That is because I know that Brimmers bitters works very nicely in each of these recipes – I have tried them all![1] Of course, there are many different brands of bitters available and many of these recipes traditionally recommend one or another product. In most cases, Angostura bitters is called for: this was the bitters I fell for in New Zealand, the bitters that Giuseppe Gonzalez had in mind when he developed the Trinidad Sour, the bitters with which every barman in New York fixes an Old Fashioned, and the bitters that the Raffles Hotel still drops into their famous Singapore Slings. In the Sazerac, Peychaud's bitters are the traditional partner – both being New Orleans natives. Products like Angostura have been around for almost 200 years and have stood the test of time for good reason – they are delicious – and thousands of bottles flood off their Trinidadian factory floor every week.

Whether you are mixing cocktails at home to show off to friends and family, or simply because you really like cocktails (or both!), it is worth the extra effort to find the best, most striking ingredients with which to furnish your drinks cabinet. In the past decade we have seen a proliferation of craft alcoholic spirits from milk vodka in Dorset to oak-aged gin in Hampshire. The bitters revolution is slowly growing. The beauty of Brimmers bitters is that each bottle has been lovingly made (in my garage in the village of Fowlmere, by my fair hands!) to a secret recipe bringing a unique flavour to your cocktails which cannot be recreated.

[1](with some help from friends – see Acknowledgments)

NOTES ON THE RECIPES

Quantities

I have tried to keep the recipes as simple as possible. Cocktail recipes often call variously for parts, ounces, or centilitre measurements, sometimes all within the same recipe. In this book I, almost universally, make reference to 'shots' or fractions thereof. In the UK a shot is 25ml or 35ml, and with a bit of luck this often matches the capacity of a cocktail shaker's lid, enabling you to use this piece of equipment for both measurement and mixing. Broadly speaking, the quantities of alcohol contained within the recipes are slightly on the conservative side as they never call for more than a single shot of any individual spirit. My simplifications and conservative conversions might be enough to worry a purist, and it will become evident that I am not one. All the measurements in this book are a guide and as such you should feel free to experiment with quantities until you have the right mix that suites your taste. Please drink responsibly.

Length and Glassware

Each cocktail is designated as short or tall. Short drinks tend to have less mixer and are served in smaller glasses like a cocktail (or Martini) glass. Tall drinks tend to have more mixer and are served in large glasses like a highball glass, or in special cases a Collins glass or Hurricane glass. Neither are exact definitions but give you a sense of what the finished recipe might look and taste like, before you embark on mixing your cocktail.

Punchiness and Booziness

Here are some inexact definitions to help you on your cocktail making way, derived from long and arduous evenings of testing with friends. (see Acknowledgements):

Punchiness

Punchiness is a measure of strength and potency. Cocktails high on the punchiness scale are likely to be sipped, rather than glugged.

Booziness

Booziness is a measure of the capacity for intoxication. Cocktails high on the booziness scale contain more alcohol or more of a mix of alcoholic components. Take care.

Examples

A cocktail like a Pink Gin sits very highly on the punchiness scale – it is after all almost entirely gin with an alcoholic content of a shade over 40%. Sipping is the order of the day. At the same time, it does just contain one shot of alcohol – no more than half a pint of beer – so it sits quite low on the booziness scale.

By contrast a Singapore Sling sits quite low on the punchiness scale – the sweet fruity notes make it really rather gluggable, especially on a warm evening. That said, the mixture of no fewer than five alcoholic components means it sits atop the booziness scale.

Each recipe in this book has a rating out of three, for both punchiness and booziness.

Bits and Pieces

You do not need much to make a good cocktail and, in most cases, a glass and a spoon will suffice. However, if you are going to invest in good ingredients, then a few items will help: a cocktail shaker (with a lid that doubles up as a shot measure), a wooden muddler for those Brimojitos™, and a metal cocktail stirrer are all that you require.

RECIPES

The recipes are divided into four, largely artificial, geographical groupings. We start in the United Kingdom before crossing the Atlantic Ocean and reaching the United States of America. We then set sail for the Caribbean and the northern shores of South America before crossing the Pacific and landing at Asia and Oceania, and even dipping a (non-alcoholic) toe into Africa.

I say these distinctions are largely artificial because the origin of most of these cocktails is often less than clear. Cocktail making hit a sweet spot around the time that modern Empires were being forged, when a gin from Plymouth could be mixed with a Curacao made in the Netherlands with Caribbean oranges and served up at a bar in Burma. By the time Jerry Thomas came to write one of the seminal cocktail books *How to Mix Drinks* in 1862, many of the recipes found in this book were already well established. As such, defining a country of origin is not always possible but we can still see which countries have staked their claim: the Rum Swizzle, for example, is often referred to as the national drink of Bermuda but some would have that it was invented on St Kitts.

In addition to complex geography, the histories behind each of the cocktails are almost always hotly contested. The Manhattan was supposedly invented for Lady Randolph Churchill at a banquet in New York, although we know she was in France and pregnant at the time of said banquet. And so on.

So the geographies are spurious, the tales are tall, the recipes themselves are endlessly debatable. But I promise they all work.

United Kingdom

JCB (JOHN COLLINS WITH BRIMMERS)

The back of any bottle of Brimmers bitters carries the Sheridan rhyme about John Collins:

My name is John Collins, head waiter at Limmer's,
Corner of Conduit Street, Hanover Square,
My chief occupation is filling brimmers
For all the young gentlemen frequenters there.

The Collins plot is a particularly thick one. There almost definitely was a John Collins (our head-waiter and hero), there might also have been a Tom Collins (but he was perhaps the same person, or never existed at all) and at some point someone saw fit to invent a Collins glass – a slightly taller and narrower version of a highball – presumably to house a Collins cocktail. Their respective stories are confusing and contradictory (like most cocktail history) and even the true parts are scarcely believable. Some will argue it was a make-believe Tom Collins (serial slanderer and part of a hoax that took in a glut of American newspapers in the 1870s) that inspired Jerry Thomas to include a 'Tom Collins' cocktail in the 1876 edition of his famous recipe book. I would say the drink was already long in existence and inspired by John Collins who was fixing drinks in London almost a century earlier. Well, anyway, it turns out that if you add a few drops of Brimmers bitters to the John Collins recipe, you are left with a wonderfully refreshing, subtly aromatic cocktail.

Length: Long
Punchiness: ★
Booziness: ★
Bits and pieces: Cocktail shaker
Glass: Collins! (or Highball)

Ingredients

1 shot dry gin
Juice of half a lemon
1 teaspoon simple syrup (see Appendix)
5 drops Brimmers bitters
Sparkling water
Lemon rind to garnish

Instructions

Pour the gin, lemon juice and syrup into a cocktail shaker, add the bitters and shake vigorously. Pour into a Collins glass filled with ice. Top up with sparkling water and garnish with the lemon rind.

Pink Gin

Purportedly a favourite tipple of the late Queen Mother, this really is the simplest of cocktails. Not for the faint of heart, Pink Gin has its origins in the Royal Navy and has a rich history of references in literature: James Bond orders one with "plenty of bitters" in the bar of the Thunderbird Hotel in Jamaica operated by Francisco "*Man with the Golden Gun*" Scaramanga, whilst Agatha Christie´s Poirot deduces that the cocktail was the source of a deadly poison in *Triangle at Rhodes*.

Length: Short
Punchiness: ***
Booziness: *
Bits and pieces: None
Glass: Old fashioned

Ingredients

1 shot Plymouth gin
6 drops Brimmers bitters
Lemon rind to garnish

Instructions

Splash a few drops of bitters into your glass and roll them around until the inside is coated. The traditional question now posed is "in or out"? You may choose whether to leave the bitters in the glass or pour out the excess leaving just the residue. Either way, add the well chilled gin, garnish with a shaving of lemon rind and serve.

Variations

The cocktail may be diluted to taste through the addition of sparkling water or, more commonly, tonic water. In this case, the drink should be served over ice in a highball glass.

Gin Pahit

Pahit being the Malay word for "bitter", some consider this to be only a linguistic variation. However, the recipe used at the Raffles Hotel in Singapore combines gin and bitters in a ratio of 3:1 giving a far more aromatic concoction.

Burnt Pink Gin

In *Drinking with Dickens*, Cedric Charles Dickens (great-grandson of Charles Dickens) records burning a teaspoon of bitters by heating over a flame before pouring into a "large tot dry gin". Do take care if you attempt to follow in Cedric´s footsteps!

Prince of Wales

A cocktail credited to Albert Edward, Prince of Wales, who would later become King Edward VII. The recipe was captured in an anonymous biography written by a member of the Royal household, *The Private Life of King Edward VII.* In our recipe we exchange powdered sugar for simple syrup, a valuable addition to any drinks cabinet.

Length: Short
Punchiness: **
Booziness: **
Bits and pieces: Cocktail shaker
Glass: Cocktail glass

Ingredients

1 shot rye whisky
1 shot Champagne
1/3 shot Maraschino liqueur
1/3 shot simple syrup (see Appendix)
5 drops Brimmers bitters
1 small piece pineapple
Lemon rind to garnish

Instructions

Measure out all the ingredients, apart from the Champagne, into a cocktail shaker along with some crushed ice. Shake vigorously before straining into a cocktail glass. Top up with Champagne, garnish with a shaving of lemon rind and serve.

Variations

King Edward VII may also have approved of the use of an agreeable English sparkling wine in lieu of Champagne.

Fallen Angel

This is the first of a trio of recipes adapted from the brilliant *Savoy Cocktail Book*, first published in 1930 and compiled by Harry Craddock, legendary head bartender at the London Hotel's "American Bar". Whilst the origin of some of these cocktails remains unknown, given the Savoy's reputation as one the UK's most iconic hotels, I have (perhaps speciously) claimed these cocktails for Britain's fair shores.

With respect to the Fallen Angel, *The Savoy Cocktail Book* notes that "*It has never been made quite clear as to whether this is intended to be taken by the Angel before or after falling; as an encouragement or as a consolation*". To my mind, this depends on how many one plans on drinking. One may serve as encouragement; more than one is likely to soften any blow.

Length: Short
Punchiness: ✱✱
Booziness: ✱
Bits and pieces: Cocktail shaker
Glass: Cocktail glass

Ingredients

1 shot dry gin
5 drops Brimmers bitters
A dash of Crème de Menthe
The juice of half a lemon
Slice of lime to garnish

Instructions

Shake the liquid ingredients, strain into a cocktail glass and serve with a slice of lime.

Variations

The original recipe calls for the juice of a whole lemon but this makes for a lip-smackingly sour drink. If you prefer, the lemon juice may be replaced with lime juice.

Ping Pong Special

Another cocktail adapted from *The Savoy Cocktail* Book featuring that most quintessentially English of cocktail ingredients: sloe gin, made from ripe sloes, traditionally picked after the first frost of winter. Numerous parts of the country hold claim to being the epicentre of the sloe-gin universe: Dorstone in Herefordshire, Hebden Bridge in West Yorkshire, and Frant in East Sussex all hold annual championships to reward the best tipple, as does Thriplow, the neighbouring village to the home of Brimmers (regretfully, I have never won a prize).

Length: Short
Punchiness: ******
Booziness: ******
Bits and pieces: Cocktail shaker
Glass: Cocktail glass

Ingredients

1 shot sloe gin
1 shot Vermouth
5 drops Brimmers bitters
Simple syrup to taste (if your sloe gin is already on the sweet side, just a dash will suffice – see Appendix)
Cherry and lemon rind to garnish

Instructions

Carefully shake the liquid ingredients together and serve with the cherry and lemon rind.

Variations

The simple syrup may be replaced with a teaspoonful of Curaçao to give an extra citrus kick.

Spencer

Our final foray into *The Savoy Cocktail Book* lands us at the Spencer Cocktail, described therein as being "very mellifluous" and with its "fine and rapid action", ideal "for morning work". As long as that work is centred on demolishing a breakfast buffet or tackling the cryptic crossword (as opposed to, for instance, operating heavy machinery) I can but agree.

Length: Short
Punchiness: ******
Booziness: ******
Bits and pieces: Cocktail shaker
Glass: Cocktail glass

Ingredients

1 shot dry gin
1/2 shot apricot brandy
5 drops Brimmers bitters
A squeeze of orange juice
A squeeze of lime juice
Cherry and orange peel to garnish

Instructions

Shake the liquid ingredients, strain into a cocktail glass and garnish with the cherry and orange peel.

Notes on the recipe

Apricot brandy can refer to an "Eau de Vie" distilled from fermented apricot juice or a liqueur made from apricot flesh and kernels. Both work nicely but if you can get hold of a true Eau de Vie like Marillenschnaps from the Wachau region in Austria you will have a wonderful addition to your drinks cabinet.

Long Vodka

A favourite north of the border, the Scots have long been known to perk up their vodka tonics with the addition of bitters. Like a Pink Gin, the bitters may be left "in or out" but for the most sharp and refreshing version, leave the bitters in!

Length: Long
Punchiness: *
Booziness: *
Bits and pieces: Cocktail shaker and stirrer
Glass: Highball

Ingredients

1 shot vodka
4 shots tonic water
5 drops Brimmers bitters
A squeeze of lime juice
Slice of lime to garnish

Instructions

Splash a few drops of bitters into a chilled highball glass and roll them around until the inside is coated. Fill with ice before adding the vodka, tonic and lime juice. Stir vigorously and garnish with a slice of lime.

Variations

The bitters may be poured away before adding the other ingredients (though this is not recommended) and the tonic water may be replaced by lemonade for a subtly sweeter cocktail.

United States of America

Old Fashioned

We begin our stateside foray with the Old Fashioned, recently brought back to prominence in the television series *Mad Men* as the cocktail of choice for the lead character, Don Draper. As ever, an exact history of the cocktail is hard to come by but its origins seem to be rooted in the Southern US with a gentlemen's club in Louisville Kentucky claiming to be first to have used the name.

Length: Short

Punchiness: ***

Booziness: *

Bits and pieces: Muddler

Glass: Old fashioned (the glass was named after the cocktail, not vice versa)

Ingredients

1 shot Bourbon or rye whisky

5 drops Brimmers bitters

1 sugar cube

Few dashes of water

Slice of orange to garnish

Instructions

Place the sugar cube in an old fashioned glass and saturate with the bitters. Add a few dashes of water. Muddle until dissolved. Fill the glass with ice cubes and add whisky. Garnish with a slice of orange.

Variations

For those less inclined to run the run the risk of undissolved sugar, David Embury in *The Fine Art of Mixing Drinks* (1948) calls for simple syrup in place of the sugar cube. One can also choose to garnish with a maraschino cherry but make too many modifications and your drink will no longer be considered an Old Fashioned.

Manhattan

Not allowing the truth to get in the way of a good story, it is possible that this cocktail began life at a party hosted by the mother of Sir Winston Churchill. It was purportedly invented at the Manhattan Club in New York City in the 1870s especially for a banquet hosted by Lady Randolph Churchill in honour of presidential candidate Samuel J. Tilden. Better to ignore the fact that Lady Randolph was likely in France and pregnant at the time of the banquet!

Length: Short
Punchiness: ★★★
Booziness: ★★
Bits and pieces: Stirrer
Glass: Cocktail glass

Ingredients

1 shot rye whisky
1/2 shot sweet red Vermouth
5 drops Brimmers bitters
Maraschino cherry to garnish

Instructions

Stir the ingredients over ice before straining into a chilled glass. Garnish with the maraschino cherry and serve "straight up" (i.e. not over ice).

Note that the ingredients can be shaken rather than stirred. Fears regarding the ingredients foaming are largely mis-held (provided your equipment is clean and ingredients pure) and traditions for both styles of preparations date back to the late 19th century.

Variations

Traditionalists insist that a Manhattan be made with American rye whisky but Bourbon may be substituted.

Rob Roy

The Rob Roy, named for the Scottish folk hero Rob Roy MacGregor, uses Scotch whisky in place of Rye.

Brooklyn

The Brooklyn, like the Manhattan, is named for one of the five New York boroughs and includes the addition of Maraschino liqueur to the above recipe.

Champagne Cocktail

Some would argue the best and only way to drink a good Champagne is poured fresh from a chilled bottle into a sparklingly clean champagne flute. David Embury puts it like this: "*no true champagne lover would ever commit the sacrilege of polluting a real vintage champagne by dunking even plain sugar – much less bitters – in it*". So, if you are lucky enough to have some vintage champagne on your wine rack, perhaps save this for another time. For a solid if unspectacular brut NV waiting to be drunk, this is a wonderful way to show off, or "*put on the dog*" in Embury's words!

Length: Short
Punchiness: **
Booziness: **
Bits and pieces: None
Glass: Champagne flute

Ingredients

Champagne
A splash of Cognac
5 drops Brimmers bitters
1 sugar cube
Maraschino cherry to garnish

Instructions

Soak a few drops of bitters onto a sugar cube and drop into a Champagne flute. Add a splash of cognac followed by gently pouring chilled champagne. Garnish with a cherry.

Do not be tempted to use loose sugar or crush the cube – the sugar is there less to sweeten the drink but more to create bubbles which the cube will do as it slowly dissolves.

Variations

Jerry Thomas's recipe omits the cognac but if you do the same, you can kiss goodbye to quoting from Raymond Chandler's *Big Sleep* where General Sternwood requests his with "*a third glass of brandy under the Champagne and the Champagne cold as Valley Forge. Colder if you can get it*"

Bourbon Lancer

If you really want the champagne to play second fiddle, the Bourbon Lancer mixes two parts Champagne to one part Bourbon with a few drops of bitters for good measure. Serve over ice with a twist of lemon peel.

Fancy

The Fancy, as detailed in *The Savoy Cocktail Book*, substitutes the sugar for a lemon syrup (simple syrup with the addition of lemon juice) which is rubbed around the edge of the glass.

Sazerac

The Sazerac came into fashion in mid nineteenth century New Orleans and was seemingly named after the brand of imported Cognac that sits at the core of this creation, *Sazerac-de-Forge et Fils*. Initially, the bitters component would likely have been provided by local apothecary, Antoine Peychaud (whose bitters you can still find today) but this will not be the first recipe that calls for a different mix: William T Boothby's seminal *The World's Drinks and How to Mix Them* (1908) called for the (now-defunct) Selner bitters. So transport yourself to 1970s New Orleans (via Cambridgeshire) and like Felix Leiter in the classic Roger Moore era bond movie, *Live and Let Die*, fix yourself a Sazerac.

Length: Short
Punchiness: ✱✱
Booziness: ✱✱
Bits and pieces: Stirrer
Glass: 2 x Old Fashioned glasses

Ingredients

1 shot Cognac
1 splash Absinthe
1 sugar cube
5 drops Brimmers bitters
Lemon peel for garnish

Method

The method here is at least as important as the ingredients, if a little fiddly (and wasteful, if you are a particular fan of Absinthe!). First take a chilled old-fashioned glass and swirl around the Absinthe to rinse the glass. Add some crushed ice and set this glass aside.

In a separate glass, stir the Cognac, bitters, sugar cube with some ice until the sugar dissolves. Now discard the ice and Absinthe from the first glass (you really only want the suggestion of aniseed) before straining the prepared mixture into this glass. Garnish with a twist of lemon.

Caribbean & Latin America

Trinidad Sour

Here is a cocktail that neatly bookends our foray stateside and sets us off in the direction of the Caribbean. The Trinidad Sour, whilst named for the island which plays home to the Angostura empire, was developed in New York by bartender Giuseppe Gonzalez and currently has a cult following on the US East Coast. The recipe is somewhat of an inversion of the standard cocktail formula with the use of a full ounce of bitters. This is not a recipe for the faint-hearted and you might want to tweak the quantities to dial down the bitterness. That said, the sweetness brought by the almond-flavoured orgeat provides a comforting reference (for me, anyway) to a classic English Bakewell pudding!

Length: Short
Punchiness: ★★★
Booziness: ★★★
Bits and pieces: Cocktail shaker
Glass: Cocktail glass

Ingredients

1 shot Brimmers bitters
1 shot orgeat
1/2 shot fresh lemon juice
1/2 shot rye whisky

Instructions

Combine the ingredients in a cocktail shaker and shake well with ice. Strain into a chilled glass and serve unadorned.

Variations

To really hammer home the pudding reference, you can add an egg white. If you do so, just remember to first shake the ingredients without ice (a so-called "dry shake") before shaking again with ice to ensure a frothy consistency.

Trinidad Especial

The Trinidad Especial, developed by Italian Valentino Bolognese, substitutes pisco for the rye whisky for a slightly different take on this already quite unusual concoction.

Planter´s Punch

Like many of the concoctions in this book, the exact history of Planter's Punch is disputed. What is clear is that it did not originate in the eponymous Planter's Hotel in Charleston, but on the rum-producing island of Jamaica some time before 1878 when it was first referred to in the London magazine, *Fun*. The recipe is notable for its hydration boosting recommendation to add "four glasses of cold water" (per jug) which I discount below in favour of ice. Humphrey Bogart would likely have approved: his character ordered one at a Panamanian bar in the 1942 spy thriller *Across the Pacific*, set on the eve of World War II.

Length: Long
Punchiness: **★★**
Booziness: **★★**
Bits and pieces: Cocktail shaker
Glass: Highball

Ingredients:

1 shot dark rum
1 shot fresh orange juice
1 shot fresh pineapple juice
1/2 shot fresh lemon juice
1/4 shot Grenadine syrup
1/4 shot simple syrup (see Appendix)
5 drops Brimmers bitters
1 small piece pineapple
Cocktail cherry to garnish

Instructions

Combine the rum, juices, syrups and bitters with ice in a cocktail shaker. Shake vigorously until well blended before pouring into a highball glass filled with ice. Garnish with a slice of pineapple and a cocktail cherry.

Variations

Whilst the recipe above closely mirrors the "official" International Bartenders' Association (IBA) recipe, this drink is a punch and, as such, the variations are endless. Different fruit juices may be incorporated - for example passion fruit or pomegranate. White rum may be substituted for or combined with the dark rum, or the rum can be skipped entirely for a delicious non-alcoholic version.

Rum Swizzle

The Rum Swizzle is often referred to as the national drink of Bermuda although, like so many of the concoctions detailed within these pages, its heritage is not without question and beverage historian Edward Emerson argued in 1909 that it originated on Saint Kitts. Rum Swizzles were on offer at what was purportedly one of the world's first cocktail parties thrown by novelist Alec Waugh, who would later write *Island in the Sun* (based on a fictitious tropical island), in 1924. Today you can head to the Swizzle Inn of Bailey's Bay, Bermuda (a favourite of island resident Michael Douglas) whose motto is "Swizzle Inn, Swagger Out". Please swizzle responsibly.

Length: Long

Punchiness: **

Booziness: **

Bits and pieces: Cocktail shaker

Glass: Cocktail glass

Ingredients

1/2 shot black rum
1/2 shot gold rum
1/2 shot lemon juice
1/ 2 shot pineapple juice
1/2 shot orange juice
1/4 shot falernum (a sweet spicy syrup used in Caribbean drinks)
5 drops Brimmers bitters
Orange peel and Maraschino cherry to garnish

Instructions

Shake the ingredients with some crushed ice in a cocktail shaker. Strain into cocktail glasses and garnish with a slice of orange and a Maraschino cherry.

Variations

Corn and Oil

Not quite a variation but a pared back counterpart, the Corn and Oil mixes 6 parts dark 'blackstrap' rum (the darker the better to give the oil-like colour) with 1 part falernum. The addition of a couple of drops of bitters adds a further depth of flavour to this simple cocktail.

Dark and Stormy

"It was a dark and stormy night…" An oft-parodied phrase that began life as the opening line to English novelist Edward Bulwer-Lytton's 1830 Novel, *Paul Clifford*. But far from *Clifford's* London, we are back in Bermuda with another cocktail that lays claim to being the island's national drink, competing with the Rum Swizzle. . Here, the "dark" is for dark rum (which should technically be Gosling Black Seal rum since it was the Gosling brothers who invented the recipe and trademarked the Dark 'N' Stormy name) and the "stormy" is for a spicy ginger beer. The original recipe stops here but at the risk of incurring the legal wrath of the Goslings, the addition of a couple of drops of Brimmers bitters rather enhances the spicy ginger notes.

Length: Long
Punchiness: *
Booziness: *
Bits and pieces: Cocktail shaker
Glass: Highball glass

Ingredients

1 shot dark rum (do not be tempted to use spiced rum)
5 drops Brimmers bitters
Ginger beer
Slice of lime to garnish

Instructions

Swirl around a couple of drops of bitters in a highball glass filled with ice. Add the rum before topping up to taste with the ginger beer and garnishing with the slice of lime.

Cuba Libre Preparado

Not to be confused with the common or garden Cuba Libre, often referred to as plain old rum and coke and invented in Cuba around the turn of the 20th century, the Cuba Libre Preparado is a grown-up version of this cocktail, popular in Venezuela. Here the addition of a splash of gin and a few drops of aromatic Brimmers bitters tone down the sweetness and provide a welcome spicy note. Whether the Venezuelans wanted a free Cuba or whether the addition of gin and bitters helped or hindered the cause has been lost to history.

Length: Long
Punchiness: **★★**
Booziness: **★★**
Bits and pieces: Cocktail shaker, stirrer
Glass: Highball glass

Ingredients

1 shot light rum
1 splash London dry gin
1 splash lime juice
5 drops Brimmers bitters
Coca-Cola
Slice of lime to garnish

Instructions

Fill a cocktail shaker about a third full with ice cubes. Add all the ingredients apart from the Coca-Cola and shake well. Strain into a highball glass filled with cracked ice. Top with the Coca-Cola, stir gently and garnish with a slice of lime.

Brimojito ™

The traditional Cuban mojito consists of five ingredients: white rum, sugar, lime juice, soda water and mint leaves. Supposedly favoured by author Ernest Hemingway, the relatively alcohol-shy mojito has grown in popularity in recent years with a report in 2014 claiming it is now the UK's favourite cocktail. Here I take inspiration from the La Fontana in Havana which serves its mojitos with a dash of bitters to cut through the sweetness. Brimmers bitters is the perfect compliment for a mojito. So good, in fact, that I have given it a new name.

Length: Long
Punchiness: ✱✱
Booziness: ✱✱
Bits and pieces: Muddler, straw, stirrer
Glass: Highball glass

Ingredients

1 shot white rum
Juice of half a lime
6 sprigs of mint
1 teaspoon of simple syrup (see Appendix)
5 drops Brimmers bitters
Soda water

Instructions

Muddle* the mint leaves (saving one for the garnish) with the sugar, lime juice and bitters. Add a splash of soda water and fill the glass with cracked ice. Pour in the rum and top with soda water. Garnish with a spare sprig of mint and serve with a straw., Stir together the liquid ingredients in a highball glass filled with ice, before garnishing with the slice of lime.

*A note on muddling

A muddler is a mixologist's pestle used to bruise leaves, not mash them into a pulp. Do not be tempted to pull out your granite number - no amount of bitters can save a cocktail full of shards of glass. Instead look like a professional by retrieving your wooden muddler from your drinks cabinet. Press gently and work in half turns.

Rest of the World

Lemon, Lime and Bitters (LLB), Non-Alcoholic

The LLB is our first non-alcoholic cocktail and a real Antipodean favourite. Some English pubs and bars may not be immediately familiar with this cocktail but most can at least feign familiarity given the strong clue to its contents in the name. In Trinidad and Tobago, where to dance is to "lime", a premixed version of this cocktail is advertised with the slogan "LLB, Lime Like a Boss"!

Length: Long
Punchiness: -
Booziness: -
Bits and pieces: Stirrer
Glass: Highball glass

Ingredients

5 parts lemonade
1 part lime cordial
5 drops Brimmers bitters
Slice of lime to garnish

Instructions

In a highball glass filled with ice, stir together the liquid ingredients before garnishing with the slice of lime.

Variations

Lime juice may be used instead of lime cordial for a slightly sharper, fresher cocktail.

Pegu Club

This was the signature drink of Burma's Pegu Club, located outside Rangoon, frequented in the main by prominent British military-men and officials prior to the country gaining independence in 1948. Named after the Pegu, a Burmese river, the drink is supposedly not easily found in present day Myanmar (I have not yet had the opportunity to independently verify this). Luckily for the rest of us, the cocktail, as Harry Craddock observed in the *Savoy Cocktail Book* in 1930, "has travelled, and is asked for, around the world."

Length: Short
Punchiness: ★★
Booziness: ★★
Bits and pieces: Cocktail shaker
Glass: Cocktail glass

Ingredients

1 shot gin
1/2 shot orange Curacao
1 teaspoooon lime juice
5 drops Brimmers bitters
Slice of lime to garnish

Instructions

Shake the ingredients together in a cocktail shaker filled with crushed ice. Strain into a chilled glass, garnish with the lime and serve.

Singapore Sling

This long drink was developed in the early 20th century by Ngiam Tong Boon, a Hainanese bartender working at the Long Bar in Raffles Hotel, Singapore. In this case, I have had the pleasure of sampling this cocktail in its place of origin. Sadly, whilst I saw fit to make a note in my journal about the unusual custom of throwing one's peanut shells on the floor, I made no note of the recipe. This is a particular shame given, as D. A. Embury notes in the *Fine Art of Mixing Drinks* "of all the recipes published for [this drink] I have never seen any two that were alike."

Length: Long
Punchiness: **
Booziness: **
Bits and pieces: Cocktail shaker
Glass: Technically a Hurricane glass but a highball will do

Ingredients

4 shots gin
2 shots cherry brandy
2 shots fresh lime juice
1 shot Cointreau
1 shot DOM Bénédictine
1 shot Grenadine
Pineapple juice
5 drops Brimmers bitters
Pineapple slice and Maraschino cherry to garnish

Instructions

Pour all the ingredients into cocktail shaker filled with ice cubes and top up with pineapple juice. Shake well before straining into a highball glass. Garnish with the pineapple and cherry.

Gunner, Non-Alcoholic

The second of our non-alcoholic cocktails, the Gunner is a much loved refreshment for expats living in parts of the Far East most likely named with reference to the colonial military presence around the time of its creation. This simple thirst-quencher is a particular favourite in the more upmarket bars of Hong Kong, a city which lays claim to its invention, but is also well suited to a warm August English evening.

Length: Long
Punchiness: -
Booziness: -
Bits and pieces: Stirrer
Glass: Highball glass

Ingredients

1 part ginger ale
1 part ginger beer
1 dash lime juice
5 drops Brimmers bitters
Slice of lime to garnish

Instructions

In a highball glass filled with ice, stir together the liquid ingredients before garnishing with the slice of lime.

Variations

The lime cordial may be exchanged for lime juice and the garnish may also be tinkered with – mint or borage flowers also work nicely.

Rock Shandy, Non-Alcoholic

The recipe for rock shandy varies across the globe but a number of versions, especially those from the African continent, include the addition of bitters. The recipe below is (supposedly) beloved in South Africa.

Length: Long
Punchiness: -
Booziness: -
Bits and pieces: Stirrer
Glass: Highball glass

Ingredients

1 part lemonade
1 part sparkling water
5 drops Brimmers bitters
Slice of lime to garnish

Instructions

In a highball glass filled with ice, stir together the liquid ingredients before garnishing with the slice of lime.

Variations

Malawi Shandy

Heading north from South Africa, it is possible to make a Malawi shady by exchanging the sparkling water for ginger beer. Think of this as the love child of a Gunner and a Rock Shandy.

Appendix

Syrups

Numerous recipes in this book call for simple syrup, a staple sweetener for a variety of cocktails. It is worth having a bottle ready to use at short notice – the long cooling time means it cannot be whipped up immediately. If you are feeling creative, this base recipe can also be readily converted to a variety of flavoured syrups.

Simple syrup

Ingredients

1 part white sugar

1 part water

You will need about 100 grams/mls of each to make 150ml of syrup.

Instructions

In a saucepan big enough for your mixture to come about a quarter of the way up the sides, bring the sugar and water to a gentle simmer, stirring the mixture occasionally to help the sugar dissolve. When the mixture comes to the boil, leave on the heat for just a few seconds before removing and allowing the mixture to cool completely. Store the syrup in an airtight container (a glass jar is perfect) and store in the refrigerator. It will last about a month or so.

Variations

Lemon syrup

At a few drops of lemon juice to make a lemon syrup, which will be useful for making a Fancy (see p25).

Acknowledgements

A big thank-you to my wife Jen for the most thorough of reviews and for putting up with Brimmers paraphernalia occasionally taking over our kitchen. To my sweet sister-in-law Philly for her guidance on a world to which I was totally unaccustomed. To Shahid Khan for turning this into something that resembles a book. To my mum, Lesley, for proof-reading, an activity to which she has applied herself gamely for more than thirty years. And to all those that shared a cocktail with me over the past few years – the Fowlmere fêters (you know who you are) and especially to Hannah, Ross, Reesie and Cat, whose commitment to experimentation on 'Japanese night' proved a vital turning point for the recipes.

Lightning Source UK Ltd.
Milton Keynes UK
UKHW02n1521241117
313291UK00003B/255/P

9 781527 213791